Preface

This book is the beginning of a series of books that address the yearning that people have to discover God's presence in the midst of their daily life.

Marc Kolden, professor of systematic theology at Luther Seminary, is a scholar who grounds his teaching in the context of the congregation. Kolden has a passion for equipping all God's people for their work in the world. With clarity and brevity, he expresses Luther's understanding of the Christian's calling.

The church often has given most of its time and attention to salvation and eternal life rather than to creation and this life. This has meant that doing ministry and living a particularly Christian life have been emphasized while people's daily lives, in all of their ordinariness and ambiguity, often haven't been linked meaningfully to faith in God. This can be frustrating for persons who spend the greatest part of their waking hours occupied with "ordinary" life.

Having a vocation or a calling from God in the world may seem strange to some Christians and others who are not accustomed to thinking about the world as being related to God. Many Christians more commonly think of God in relation to the world *to come* rather than to this world; they do not think much about God's involvement in the present but mostly about the promised future eternal life. Yet the Bible doesn't split things up that way. The Bible portrays God as the giver of new life, as the one who creates *and* who redeems and restores the creation.

The intent of this book is to address this problem by giving some concepts and illustrations to help Christians and perhaps others deepen and widen their understanding of what it means to have a "divine" vocation, a calling from God, in and for this present world.

How to use this book:
    The first part of the book, "An Understanding of Christian Vocation," is a clear, brief summary of Martin Luther's work on vocation. The second part, "The Christian's Calling in the World," originated as an practical essay for Christians on the idea of "vocation" or the idea that God calls people to have certain roles and responsibilities in their lives in the world. It is divided into five brief chapters, each followed by questions for individual or small group reflection in a congregation or by people who share common interests or occupations.

ISBN 0-9742283-0-3

Table of Contents

An Understanding Of Christian Vocation

The Christian's Calling in the World

An Understanding Of Christian Vocation

One of the 16th century Reformation's greatest contributions to the Christian church was its teaching on vocation. This teaching—that one had a calling from God in whatever circumstances one lived—gave meaning to the daily life of every Christian, not only to those with religious vocations.

The History of the Idea of Vocation

The term "vocation" is simply the Latin form of the word for "call." In the New Testament the word "call" is used primarily to refer to the call to follow Jesus or the call to believe the gospel. This remains its first meaning for Christians, as when in Martin Luther's Small Catechism (The Explanation to the Third Article of the Creed), we say that the Holy Spirit has **called** us through the gospel. But "vocation" and "calling" came to have other meanings as well, and it is these that we must consider.

As the Christian church became larger during the centuries following the New Testament, many people became Christians who did not seem very serious about it. This was especially true when Christianity became the official religion of the Roman Empire and everyone was expected to belong to the church. Reform movements, especially monastic movements, began to speak of those who were called to a higher righteousness, who were expected to keep not only the Ten Commandments but all of Jesus' teachings, and who therefore had "higher" callings. "Vocation" became a word referring primarily to monks, nuns, and priests, while ordinary Christians were taught that they did not have divine vocations. To make matters worse, a growing trend among Christians to speak as if salvation came not by grace through faith (as the New Testament and the great teachers of the early church had taught) but by faith and good works led Christians to look upon monastic vocations as a way of gaining salvation rather than of being of service to God and God's world. The great Reformer Martin Luther began his career as a monk in Germany at the time when such works righteousness was at its peak.

Luther's Teaching on Vocation

Martin Luther was born in 1483 in eastern Germany. By the time he was 35 years old (1518) he had become a very dedicated monk and had received a doctor's degree in biblical studies. But he had also experienced the inadequacy of a system that taught that a person could become righteous before God by doing the works of prayer and devotion that the monastic vocation required. Luther's study of the Bible revealed to him a completely different way to become right with God: that God in Christ has done everything that was necessary for our salvation and that we receive this by faith alone, not by doing something to achieve it. Luther's discovery of the gospel (that is, the "good news" that God was in Christ reconciling the world) led him to have to rethink the whole of the Christian life.

If doing religious works was not the route to achieving salvation, then why was he a monk? If salvation was all God's doing and not the result of human achievements, then why did the church teach that Christians with religious vocations had a higher status than those who lived ordinary lives in the world? If salvation was by faith alone, then what was the place of good works? If righteousness came by the gospel, then what was the place of the law? Such questions were at the heart of Luther's reformation of the Christian life.

The monastic system was the first thing to go. It made no sense to speak as if persons who were preoccupied with religious disciplines, spiritual pilgrimages, exaggerated self-denial, and repetitive worship had special callings if salvation was a gift of God, received by faith alone. Then what is the place of good works? Luther saw from the Bible that good works are commanded by God, so they are not optional. But what makes them good is not that they are done for God but that they serve people in need. Luther said, "A good work is good for one's neighbor." Good works are not for eternal life but for this life, here and now. God commands them because God loves this world and wants to get it loved through our good works.

Loving one's neighbor was not Luther's new idea. Christians of every age had at least paid lip service to love. What Martin Luther saw that was so radical was the way in which love for the neighbor was to be expressed. *If God in Christ saves us by faith alone, setting us free from doing works in order to achieve our salvation, God does this so that our works can be directed where they are needed-to our neighbors. But where will this happen? In a monastery? Not likely.* But in our families and communities? Yes. In our school and work? Yes. In government and business? Yes. In our many roles in daily life? Yes. Precisely there. And so Luther took that word, "vocation," meaning divine calling, and applied it to all Christians in all their roles and places of responsibility:

> How is it possible that you are not called? You have always been in some state or station; you have always been a husband or wife, or boy or girl, or servant. Picture before you the humblest estate. Are you a husband, and you think you have not enough to do in that sphere to govern your wife, children, domestics, and property so that all may be obedient to God and you do no one any harm? Yea, if you had five heads and ten hands, even then you would be too weak for your task, so that you would never dare to think of making a pilgrimage or doing any kind of saintly work.
> (From one of Martin Luther's sermons.)

This insight, that one serves God by doing the sort of works that our various places in life require of us, made love exceedingly **concrete**. It took love out of so-called spiritual areas and related it to service to one's neighbor in what seemed to be very ordinary ways: raising children, caring for elderly parents, farming, participating in government, paying taxes, going to school. Every Christian, from the least to the greatest, from the youngest to the oldest, could now be seen to have a divine calling. This was the case because God creates and sustains the world that we sometimes call "ordinary," and God wants to see to it that this world is cared for and therefore calls each one of us to be involved in such care.

The idea of divine callings in daily life spread rapidly among many Protestant groups because it fit so well with the idea that we are all sinners who are saved by God's grace alone in order that we can be set free to live as faithful creatures and stewards in the world God has made. No longer would it be said that kings and bishops and the rich were more blessed by God than the common people; because of Christ we are all equal in God's eyes (as forgiven sinners) and we all have divine callings.

In order to make his point, Luther often pointed to rather common situations in life that had been downgraded by a church that exalted monastic vocations. Marriage and occupation were two roles that Luther held up instead. He made his point so well that later Christians have sometimes thought (wrongly) that one had to be married and work for pay to have a divine calling. In fact, in our day the word "vocation" is often equated with an occupation. But that was not Luther's meaning: occupation was included in vocation, but vocation was much broader than that. People without occupations, such as children and retired or unemployed persons, still were said to have vocations—that is, ways in which they could serve God in their situations by serving their neighbors. Children serve by being responsible members of their families and by going to school, for example. Such things are their callings. Elderly persons serve in many ways even when they are no longer employed: for example, by caring for others, paying taxes, being responsible citizens, volunteering, being the focus of the love of others, praying, etc.

This comprehensive view of vocation is very important in any contemporary reappropriation of the doctrine of vocation, so that we will not reduce it only to occupation, on the one hand, and so that we will see that it is set within the broad parameters of God's creative and sustaining work, on the other.

 ## God's Law

The idea of God's law is important here. If God's law is God's will, both as that is expressed in divine commands and as it is built into the way God has created the world, then God's law will be closely related to how our lives are ordered in this world. This means, first, that there are some criteria available from the Bible as to how we live out our roles in daily life (for example, not killing, not stealing, etc.). But, second, it also means that God's law will stand over any specific human or societal standards of conduct if these latter might lead us to do things that are not loving to our neighbors; many things that society holds to be legal or acceptable may look quite different when viewed according to God's law.

Finally, in light of God's saving work in Jesus Christ, we must realize that the law is not God's only word for any situation. The gospel brings forgiveness and freedom from the law's accusation of us, it promises newness of life that gives us hope beyond what we can accomplish, and it reminds us that the God who gives the law must always be understood as the God who was in Christ, a God of justice and mercy. The gospel sets us free from the law's condemnation and it sets us free to seek the good of our neighbor—which is, after all, the true purpose of God's law.

Vocation and Sanctification

A final matter in considering the meaning of Christian vocation is Luther's notion of the death of the sinful self in our callings. If we believe that Jesus Christ died for sinners, an implication of this is that people's sin must be very serious. Nothing less than the death of God's son on the cross could save us. And if we believe that this salvation comes as a gift to us when our sins are forgiven for Jesus' sake, then (Luther saw) it means that even when we are pardoned and counted righteous, in ourselves we still remain sinful. That is what "pardon" means: that the one who is in the wrong is nevertheless not punished but is considered to be not guilty. This led Luther to draw from Paul's writings in the New Testament the idea that the Christian is both sinful and righteous at the same time: while in Christ (in faith) we are new and righteous, in ourselves we are old and sinful. "Old" and "new" here are used in a particular way by the Bible, which speaks both of "this age" and "the age to come" and claims that in Jesus Christ the age to come has already begun in this age. As we follow Christ now, we participate in both ages, we are both "old" and "new." One of the tasks of God's Spirit between now and eternity is to put to death our sinful self so that only our self which is one with Christ will remain.

It should be added at this point that when we speak of our "sinful self," we do not mean that in ourselves we are only sinful. The created life that God constantly gives us is very good, just as God judged it to be in Genesis. But it is also sinful, as the story of the fall into sin reminds us. Sin, rooted in unbelief in God's Word that it is good to be a finite, mortal, human creature, constantly causes us to defect, to misuse our good life. That defection permeates every part of us and every thought and action—even our very highest and best ways of living. Jesus took on flesh to restore our true creatureliness by putting an end to the rule of sin in us. His judgment was not on our humanness but on our sinfulness. It is important to remember this when we speak of "putting to death the sinful self" or we may hear this phrase as a creation-denying or life-denying word rather than one that affirms God-given creatureliness.

The Holy Spirit puts the sinful self to death by means of God's law, which not only commands us to love our neighbors but at the same time (because we are sinful and tend to love ourselves at the expense of others) always accuses us of our lack of love. This accusing and condemning function of God's law, whether it comes from preaching and teaching of God's word or from the demands built into the very structures of our lives, finally leaves us without a leg to stand on before God. It culminates in our actual physical death, which leaves us both unable to sin and completely dependent on God and his power to raise us from death.

This idea is at least somewhat familiar to students of the New Testament, but it is easily spiritualized to refer to "mortification" (putting to death) by punishing oneself through fasting, physical suffering, or psychological disciplines. Luther had experienced all of these in his monastic life, and he found them to be self-centered and ultimately unhelpful. This led him to see that the obvious way for the Holy Spirit to put the sinful self to death by the law is precisely in those places where we live according to the law—in our callings in daily life. Here, in seeking to love our neighbors, the self-centered self will be limited, the unloving self will be led or forced to do loving deeds, and the despairing self will be called to constructive actions.

This means that for Luther the teaching of Christian vocation is absolutely central not only for ethics but also for the way God works to save us. If we (wrongly) think that faith means only correct "belief" and does not involve us in works of love, then we do not have faith—because faith is trusting God with all our heart and soul and mind and strength. Faith is a total rearrangement of life that occurs when Christ comes to us and calls us to follow. Faith without works is not faith! The gospel without vocation is not the gospel because it simply leaves us at ease in our old sinful self—which Christ does not do. He loves us more than that, so he forgives us and gives us callings in daily life—both for the good of others and for our own eternal good.

There is a "cross" in every vocation, Luther said. The cross is the means by which God puts to death the sinful self through the demands for service wherever we are. We do not have to seek such a cross; it will find us. We do not glory in such a cross; for we are ashamed of our sin that makes it necessary. But we must not conceal this whole dimension of God's saving work on us when we speak of Christian vocation or we risk misleading ourselves both about salvation (that it is easy or cheap rather than free) and about vocation (that when one is a Christian life is automatically meaningful or free of struggle and failure).

To put it another way, speaking of the cross in vocation that puts to death the sinful self is the most appropriate way to think of "sanctification" for a theological tradition that confesses as its central teaching that we are justified by faith alone. Being sanctified by the death of the sinful self, worked by God's Spirit, is a way of understanding that makes it clear that sanctification is no more a human achievement than is justification.

Conclusion

I n order to retrieve the Reformation's doctrine of Christian vocation in our day, we will need also to retrieve a dynamic view of God's ongoing creative work (as the Bible portrays it and as Luther expounded it). If we do not do this, vocation can become static and oppressive. We also must not allow vocation to be governed only by God's law (or the law as it is built into society) without keeping it connected also with the gospel. Since faith is created by the gospel, the gospel is essential both in seeing "reality" in the larger terms of God's creative and redeeming work and in supplying criteria for making judgments about the demands of our callings so that we do not use them as ways of escaping God's will and only serving ourselves. Finally, we need the gospel's promised forgiveness to give us the freedom to enter into the ambiguity and messiness of daily life without having to worry about our own righteousness or reputation but only about the good of the neighbor. With these reminders, the idea of Christian vocation can be a fruitful and joyful way of approaching life and one that leads to constructive and transformative action in the world.

Selected Bibliography

Wingren, Gustaf. 1957. *Luther On Vocation*. Philadelphia: Muehlenberg Press, 1957. The best work on Luther's views, it relates vocation to his whole theological framework and helps avoid misuse of this doctrine in some of the static and selfserving ways that have sometimes occurred in Protestant history.

Hardy, Lee. 1990. *The Fabric of This World: Inquiries into Calling, Career Choice, and the Design of Human Work*. Grand Rapids, MI, Eerdmans, 1990. An excellent recent treatment of both Luther and Calvin on vocation, with sections on career choice and ways of humanizing work situations.

Heiges, Donald. 1984. *The Christian's Calling*. Philadelphia: Muehlenberg Press, 1984.

Benne, Robert. 1988. *Ordinary Saints*. Philadelphia: Farress Press, 1988. Both Heiges and Benne are helpful introductory treatments of these topics.

The Christian's Calling
in the World

God's Work in Creation

How are Christian believers to live appropriately in the world of daily life, the world we call "secular," and how do we think that God is related to that world? What follows is a proposal for a way of thinking that is true to the Bible and to the heritage of the sixteenth-century Protestant Reformation—a "framework" to help Christians make sense of and live in the exciting and daunting world of the early twenty-first century.

First, to speak of life in the natural and social world a Christian must speak of the doctrine of *creation*. The Christian doctrine of creation says that nothing exists with which God is not involved. The biblical understanding of creation tells us that in our daily life we have to do with God because God gives daily life and this earth and our neighbors and even our social structures. God gives these in part through human activity, but it is still *God* who gives all these things, according to the Bible.

The most important point for us to remember is that the biblical view of creation is *not* that "once upon a time" God created these things and now they just run of their own accord. The Bible says that not only did God create in the beginning but that in every moment God is creating, that each of us and everything in the world depends upon God continually creating and preserving or we and everything else would cease to be. Martin Luther knew this: in his Catechism he speaks of the God who "has created and *still preserves* my eyes and ears and all my powers" and who "daily provides abundantly" for all the needs of my life. Psalm 104 is the most vivid portrayal of this; the whole Psalm is about God's creative work and most of the verbs—the action words—are in the *present* tense.

We often forget this and are misled in our thinking and speaking. For example, we may say about someone that "she doesn't have a relationship with God." What we probably mean is that this person doesn't believe in God, but it is dead wrong to say that someone isn't related to God; people wouldn't be alive if God weren't relating to them in every moment. A famous preacher once said that you can tell if God is working in your life if your nose works! (He got that also from Psalm 104.)

Another thing we often say is that "God works through the church." Of course. That is a good thing to say, *but* we sometimes seem to imply that God isn't working anyplace else. And that is dead wrong again. God is constantly at work in the whole world, not only in the church or among believers. One of our tasks as Christ's followers is to proclaim the truth about God so that all those in and through whom God is working but who don't know it yet may hear and believe.

Second, why is it important to put so much emphasis on God's creative work? Because it doesn't make much sense to speak of our callings in the world if the world has nothing to do with God. If the world were godless or totally secular, then why would we have any divine callings there at all? Yet in our time that is how many people, including many believers, think about the world. We call it "a godforsaken place." Or, our experience of life's trials and pain is so great that we think God must be somewhere else. Or, sin is so prominent in the world—just watch the evening news—that we can't see how the world can belong to God.

And there is truth in those feelings. We can't deal with the world *only* as God's good creation, even though the most important thing the Bible says about all of God's creative work is that it is "very good"—and that even includes God's verdict on each of us (Gen. 1:31). Yet we all know that this is not the whole story. The Bible also speaks of *sin*. And again, when it speaks of sin, it doesn't just speak of "once upon a time." The apostle Paul wrote that "all [of us] have sinned and fall short of the glory of God" (Rom. 3:23). It's not as simple as saying that Adam and Eve sinned long ago and the rest of us have simply inherited it; that would make sin into a kind of birth defect that is not our responsibility. Rather, Paul treats Adam as a *type*, a pattern of us all, and he says that "in Adam" we all sinned (see Rom. 5:12-14). Not only by an action or two but by falling into bondage, into a faithless propensity to sin in every aspect of our lives. We humans, the crown of God's creation, beings who are only a little less than God (Ps. 8), have by our sin put the whole natural world into bondage to sin so that it "groans" until we are finally set free (Rom. 8:21-23).

Therefore, sin is a very important qualifier of the world's goodness. Yet we shouldn't let our belief in the seriousness of sin make us forget that God still creates anew each day and that everything that comes from God is good—even though we constantly pervert it. This is true for human beings as well: that which we are essentially—human—*is good*, even though we constantly misuse and demean our own humanness. The point here is this: for the Bible the existence of sin is never a reason to abandon the world, as some Christians mistakenly have thought. God's still gives us roles, duties, tasks, relationships, responsibilities, opportunities, and challenges precisely in the world; and God gives us the commandments and other words, our own reason and abilities, and our societal institutions and communities to aid us in living in the world. Our faith helps us see this and sets us free and motivates us to serve in the world.

Third, we need to ask how this emphasis on God's creative work relates to our salvation in Jesus Christ. Sometimes Christians have thought (wrongly) that salvation is an escape from the world—a flight to heaven, a preoccupation with the "spiritual" over the material, a retreat to religion away from daily life. But this does not fit with the way the Bible portrays God's saving act in sending Jesus Christ.

Jesus came because God so loved the *world*; he took on *flesh* and became truly *human*; he came that we might have abundant *life*; and our eternal hope is for the resurrection of our *bodies* and for a new heaven and a new *earth*. Jesus enacted what was always true: that God is a "down-to-earth" God. Our sin is when we flee the earthly and our humanness, our neighbors and our callings in daily life. Our sin is when we don't believe God's word that it is good to be a human creature and instead seek to rise above our creatureliness and "lord it over" others or (conversely) to sink beneath our human status and flee from freedom and responsibility into mere sensate existence (giving in to despair, drugs, cynicism, conformity, or whatever).

Redemption through Christ is to reclaim and restore, and complete and fulfill, the creative work of God—not to abandon it. Christianity first of all is about life, not religion. Jesus said that he came that people might have abundant *life* (John 10:10). He declared that the sabbath was made for people, not people for the sabbath (Mark 2:27). Believing in Christ and receiving the forgiveness of our sins sets us free to be faithful *creatures*, people who can believe once again that this life is good because it comes from God, who can see other people not merely as competitors or "pains in the neck" or interruptions or enemies but as *neighbors*. In faith we see other people as those through whom God comes to us and to whom God comes through us.

When we are in Christ we are new creations (2 Cor. 5:17). We are restored to play a role in God's world, even in the midst of our own and the world's sin. One of the temptations of Jesus in the Bible (Matt. 4:1-11) was to worship the devil as the "ruler of this world;" but to give into this temptation would have been for Jesus to "let the world go to the devil," even though the world actually belongs to God. This very well may be our temptation also, especially in difficult times, but here we are well advised to stick with Jesus, in whom *God* was, reconciling the world to himself, not letting it go to the devil.

Questions to think about and discuss:

1. Did you learn anything new in this lesson? What things?

2. Were you reminded of some things you once knew but had forgotten? What?

3. Read Psalm 104, paying special attention to the verbs. Is the way that God is portrayed in this Psalm how you usually think of God?

4. Which claims of this lesson, if any, do you have some questions about or do you disagree with or do you find confusing? Remember these in order to see whether the next lessons address them.

Good resources for thinking about ourselves as God's creatures in God's creation are Martin Luther's Small and Large Catechisms, especially the explanations to the first article of the Apostles' Creed and the petition of the Lord's Prayer to "Give us this day our daily bread."

God's Work *through* Us

N ow we must get more specific about what it means that we have divine callings in the world. Here we can benefit greatly from Martin Luther's insights because his understandings of faith and life were developed in a situation of struggle and conflict about the very heart of the Christian life. His new understanding of the Christian's worldly *calling* (or "vocation," the Latin form of the same word) became central for him, in contrast to his previous calling as a monk. Even in the midst of the harshness of life in the early sixteenth century, with wars, plagues, poverty, and oppression, Luther rejuvenated the biblical teaching of God's ongoing, ever-present creative work. Not that God *controls* everything—humans are given a certain amount of freedom and responsibility for things on earth—but that since God gives all life, God is involved in some way in everything. As Luther portrays it, God's work is very concrete: God gives new babies through fathers and mothers; God raises children through parents, other family members, and teachers; God creates food through farmers and soil and sun and rain, and then through millers and butchers and processors and distributors. Even if people don't realize it, they serve God as God works through them in their lives, relationships, and roles, using their activity and abilities to keep the world going and bless its inhabitants.

How did Luther come to think this way? And might it make sense for us? It all followed from his major discovery that we are saved by faith in Christ and not by doing good works for God (which then were supposed to cause God to judge us to be righteous and then reward us with salvation). Luther saw in the New Testament that good works (or "works of law") have no role in gaining our salvation. Christ does it all and for his sake God graciously forgives our sins and gives us faith, new life, and salvation. So then, Luther asks, "What is the role of good works?" He answers that when God in Christ sets us free *from* worrying about achieving our own salvation God also sets us free to live life on this earth in ways that are faithful to our being God's beloved creatures in the world. Then we know in faith that God works through us to do his will and that our good works are one of God's means of caring for the whole creation.

This would seem to be quite clear, but many followers of the reformers have gotten it mixed up. They have talked a lot about being saved or "justified" by faith, but they have wrongly thought that this means that God arbitrarily decided to save those who believed in the *doctrine* of justification by faith rather than those who believed they were justified by doing works. That is crazy thinking! God has a *reason* and it is this: God does not need our good works. All the monastic practices that Luther rejected—religious exercises, buying indulgences, saying a thousand prayers, fasting (things also urged on the laity in general and not only on the monks)—didn't do anything for God and, even worse, they kept people from doing useful works for the good of other people. Luther saw what the apostle Paul had been talking about in the first place: that God saves us by faith in Christ and not by works *so that* our works can be directed toward those who really need them—our neighbors. (And a "neighbor" is anyone in need, as the parable of the Good Samaritan shows us [Luke 10:25-37].)

To put this in strict doctrinal terms: Christ frees us *from* seeking to keep God's law as a means of achieving salvation and he frees us *for* living according to the law as a means of benefiting others by promoting good and opposing evil. This latter is what Luther called the "first" or *civil* use of the law, for the good of life in the world. Luther highly praises this use of the law. However, if one tries to use keeping the law as a way of gaining salvation, then Luther spoke of the law's "second" or *accusing* use, because the law will always *also* reveal our sin of not keeping it fully or gladly, of not loving our enemies or our neighbors as ourselves, and then the law will accuse us. Luther located the Christian's calling or vocation in the sphere of the first or civil use of the law. Of course, he also realized that anytime we deal with the law its second or accusing use will be close at hand. (We will come back to this later.)

How did Christians in Luther's time respond to his insights? At first, they were puzzled because it was almost exactly the opposite of what they had always been taught. It had become clear to Luther because of his own experience. He had been caught up in the monastic system that taught that the only people who had real callings to serve God were those in full-time religious service—especially monks and nuns and also parish priests. But when Luther rediscovered the apostle Paul's insight that salvation is by grace through faith, apart from works, he realized that it is completely backwards to say that the only people who have divine callings are those who seek to gain salvation by works! So he took the same word, "calling" or "vocation," and applied it instead to ordinary Christians. He said that it was not the professionally religious who had callings from God but rather *all* believers have divine callings. In fact, he added, most of the activities that the professionally religious were engaged in at that time should not be named "callings" at all because they are of little or no *earthly* good. Luther took vocation out of the religious realm, where works have no value, and put it into daily life—the only place where works matter.

People who had thought that they were only second-class Christians, and who thought that they only served God when they attended worship or prayed or gave money, were astonished to hear that when the gospel called them to faith it also revealed that *all* the activities of their lives were areas in which God was calling them to serve and in which God wanted to work through them. Aspects of life that previously had seemed merely matters of circumstance or birth (e.g., race, gender, nationality, appearance, aptitude, family situation, age, occupation, citizenship, etc.) were given a new interpretation. These ordinary things were all ways in which God had given them life and where they could and should serve God by being faithful creatures; that is, faithful to what that aspect of life asked of them. Doing so would enable God to work through them in regular, reliable, and effective ways.

One does not have to become a monk or a nun, Luther said; one does not have to go on a pilgrimage to Rome or to some other holy place; one does not have to retreat from the world. Listen to his words from a sermon he preached in the local parish church to Christian laity:

> How is it possible that you are not called? You have always been in some state or station; you have always been a husband or wife, a boy or girl, or servant. Picture before you the humblest estate. Are you a husband, and you think you have not enough to do in that sphere to govern your wife, children, domestics, and property so that all may be obedient to God and you do no one any harm? Yea, if you had five heads and ten hands, even then you would be too weak for your task, so that you would never dare to think of making a pilgrimage or doing any kind of saintly work. (From the Lenker edition of Luther's Works, v. 10, p. 242.)

Note that by "calling" or "vocation" Luther does not only mean one's occupation. It sometimes has come to mean that in our society (as in Vocational Technical Schools), but that is much too narrow. Luther called people's occupations "vocations" primarily to make the point that all the Christian's activities in the world can be places where we serve God, even daily work. He made this point against a religious system that had denigrated secular occupations and primarily emphasized religious roles. For the same reason Luther emphasized the calling of marriage and having children, in contrast to the monastic ideal of celibacy. In actuality, Luther's view of divine callings was exceedingly broad, including being students, children, government officials, citizens, elderly, and all sorts of other private and public roles and activities. We in our time should not make the opposite mistake of so exalting as divine callings only occupations and marriage that these become new forms of works righteousness and suggest that single people or the unemployed do not have divine callings—exactly the opposite of what Luther was saying.

All Christians have callings to serve God by seeking the common good in every aspect of life in which they find themselves or which they choose to enter. Notice that this is not to claim that God calls anyone only to certain tasks; nor is it necessary that persons stay forever in the same sort of work or role in order for God to work through them. Luther's point is: wherever we are, there we are called. Only if we absolutely cannot serve God there, or God cannot work through us there— since some occupations, roles, and relationships do not allow one to love one's neighbor—must we change. In saying this, Luther again was broad in his intention, not limiting love to the neighbor only to uplifting or sacrificial types of service, but seeing even the most common acts as part of God's working through people if these acts were for the neighbor's or society's good.

It is important at this point to address a common criticism made of Luther's ideas on vocation. He often quoted the advice of the apostle Paul in 1 Corinthians that Christians should stay in the situation in which they were called (1 Cor. 7:20, 24). Paul wrote this because he believed that it would be only a very short time until Christ returned, so changing one's situation didn't make much sense. However, when Luther used the same passages he did so in order to assure Christians that they did not have to go *elsewhere* to serve God, such as to a monastery or on a religious pilgrimage. Later Lutherans and others sometimes took Luther's words out of his context and wrongly interpreted him to have said that people needed to stay in their place and not change roles, occupations, or situations— especially if they were lower class, or children, or women. These interpreters made Luther sound as if he favored a static society in which injustice and inequity were simply accepted and harmful class distinctions were endorsed. Yet it should be obvious from what has been said previously that this is not what Luther was saying; his view of the world and of the Christian life was much more dynamic than that, especially because of his biblical view of God's ongoing creative, preserving, and renewing work.

Questions to think about and discuss:

1. What do you think about the idea that God works even through people who don't believe in God?
2. Does the idea of our being justified (=made right with God) through faith in Jesus Christ and not by what we do fit with your own relationship with God? Why or why not?
3. This lesson says that God calls believers in our work and other activities in ordinary daily life and that these roles and responsibilities are our "callings" or "vocations." What do you think about this? Do you find it believable? Do you find it helpful?
4. Are there specific areas in your life that you have thought of as divine callings (that is, places God calls you)? Are there some new areas that this lesson suggests might also be divine callings for you? Can you think of any aspects of your life (now or previously) in which you do not think God would call you?
5. Has this lesson challenged any of your previous ideas? Which ones? And why?

For further reading, see the books and articles listed at the end of this book.

Our Work *with* God

N ow, let's look at some examples of how we might think about our callings in God's world. Suppose you are an adult who is fortunate enough to be employed for pay. In faith you will see your occupation not only as a means of making a living or of building your career or of being able to do other things, such a traveling or buying a boat, but above all you will see your job as a means by which God keeps the world going and gets other people loved (including your family, if you have one, but many other people as well). If your work is teaching, for example, then the love you are to show to your neighbors (students, their parents, staff, school board, community, others) is not only or primarily that you are nice to them but that you teach your students things that are true and useful and important for living in God's world. That might be auto-mechanics, math, literature, nursing, computer science, or even theology! The point is that God works through you as a teacher to equip others so that God will be able to work through them also.

Or, suppose that you work in a business. Serving your customers accurately and efficiently and serving your fellow employees and the business itself so that it is profitable are obviously important. And this helps the business serve the community in which the business is located and less directly the nation and the world. All these are fairly obvious parts of the job for believers and non-believers alike. But as a believer in God, you will understand that in all of these ways you are also serving God by helping to keep God's world going and providing in various ways for those in need. This awareness also may lead you to make certain decisions rather than others in your work or to work harder than you otherwise would have. It may even lead you to challenge certain practices or policies of the business or of the laws that govern it. The point is that in all of these ways you are working with the God who calls you in this role.

If one of your callings is being a member of a family (whether as child, parent, grandparent, spouse, sibling, in-law, or whatever) then that too is a role and relationship in which God is served as we care for and about other family members. Or if you are a farmer, while being able to make a living economically obviously is very important, it cannot be your only or primary goal if you understand what you do to be part of God's work of feeding the world's people and of contributing to the surrounding community. At a time when family farming in North America is becoming more and more difficult, simply knowing that one serves God also by farming will not in itself solve the problems, to be sure. But it will put farming in a larger context than only the political or economic aspects to which farm problems often are reduced, because it will take people, the environment, the affected communities, and matters of justice more seriously. On the other side, confidence in God's goodness and steadfast love may be what frees people from making an idol out of farming (or any other occupation or way of life) when it is necessary to think about other ways of working with God.

Looking at life in terms of our being called by God opens up our situations for thinking in terms of God's will and God's presence in ways which otherwise probably would not happen. This may result in some new directions or solutions; it may give us encouragement and patience or resolve and perseverance; or it may help us to call it quits in some role without thinking that there is no other place in which God could call us. Someone has said very wisely: Respond to every action upon you as if it includes also God acting upon you. We still have to interpret what God might be doing in such cases; we still have to make decisions and take actions; but we will do so confident that the God who comes to us through faith in Jesus Christ is involved in the seemingly mundane and often difficult aspects of daily life.

A point that Martin Luther often makes, that probably surprises us, is that while most occupations and other roles in life are good because they are created by God, at the same time the devil attacks us precisely in these good callings in order to lead us astray, to lead us away from serving the good of others and instead tempts us to seek only our own good. This can happen in many ways, according to Luther. The devil might tempt us to think that God may not have (or surely could not have) called us to a particular role we have and would urge us to leave it, perhaps because it is not pure enough or it is not worthy of our abilities. But giving in to that temptation also might mean leaving neighbors whom God needs us to love. To be sure, some invitations to move to a new job or another situation rightly will be seen as God's call; but the devil is subtle and seeks to deceive us in many ways—whether in staying or leaving. That is Luther's point. Certainly much TV programming and advertising can be means that the devil uses to promote values and ways of living that undermine what God calls us to do, even though TV can also inform of us many important events and ideas. The multiplication of lotteries and gambling could be seen as a way that the devil tempts us to seek to become rich, which would have as one of its results that we would quit our jobs (and the neighbors we serve there) and live only for our own pleasure. Would God call anyone to enter the lottery? Yet millions of people are answering someone's call to do so. We must not be naive when we serve God in worldly callings.

As might be obvious from all of these examples, simply believing in Jesus Christ and believing that we are called to serve him in our roles in daily life will not automatically tell us *what* we are to do or *how* we are to do it. The Bible does not teach us how to cut hair or raise corn or run a computer; and though it does say some things about being parents and citizens and about responding to humans in crisis situations, even there faith by itself may not give us enough guidance. Martin Luther was pretty clear about this: the gospel of Jesus Christ has to do with our salvation; it is not to be used to run the world. Over the centuries some Christians have tried to run the world according to the gospel, by creating exclusive Christian communities or by trying to put gospel practices (e.g., loving one's enemies) into society directly, but such experiments have usually been very strange, if not disastrous, and have ended up back in works righteousness—suggesting that if you do not live in a certain way, then you aren't a "real" Christian.

Luther's point was that God rules the world through the law or divine commands (and not through the gospel); and he understood commands or law to be not only the Ten Commandments or the two Great Commandments but what he called "natural law," by which he meant God's will built right into the world itself and available to be known to some extent through human reason. If God's will is part of God's creative work, when it comes to our helping to keep the world going and our neighbors loved we will be able to rely on the insights and knowledge that are available in the world and to all who can think—and not only to believers. For example, we do not learn a language or how to operate a machine primarily by praying; rather, we go to school or take lessons and we study and practice. We do not simply preach the gospel to people so that they will be good, but we pass laws and enforce them, knowing that people are not only capable of good but also are sinful. It may be that a non-believer or a member of another religion learns faster or is better at something than a Christian is. All people are God's creatures, after all, and according to Romans 1-2 all people have some knowledge of God's will. The difference will be that Christians know that in dealing with the world we are also dealing with the God we know through Jesus Christ and this gives us some clues as to what God might be up to—not the least of these being God's law.

Some Christians, including many Lutherans, have thought that we should only say bad things about God's law. But the law is only bad when it intrudes into our salvation, when we think God only saves us or forgives us when we do so many good things that we deserve salvation. Then the law is bad because it tempts us to think that Jesus' crucifixion for our sins was unnecessary. And that same law will turn on us, revealing our sin (where we have broken the law, where we have hated what the law commands, or even hated the One who gave the law) and driving us into despair or rebellion against God. That is why Luther and others often have said bad things about God's law—because sinners get it all messed up. But *on earth*, in daily life, Luther said, the law is the most wonderful thing in all creation; in fact, he even says that on the human and historical level we can be justified by keeping the law! That is, in society we correctly judge some people to be "righteous" or "good" on the basis of their achievements or character or their principles. And we correctly condemn others because of their hateful or vicious or thoughtless actions or statements. *On earth* these conclusions, based on our knowledge of God's law, are important. Life would be chaos without them. With this clarification, we can get back to the positive ways the law works in our callings.

If God's law in some ways is God's own will built right into the whole creation, this means that we will know God's will in a certain situation by the demands of our role itself. If you are a parent, for example, God's will in many ways will be defined by what is required of a parent (interpreted in faith, to be sure, but with help from psychology, hygiene, nutrition, common sense, and the like). An infant screams to be fed and expresses God's will; the parent feeds the child and does God's will. The child loves being loved, held, played with, being sung to, being told stories; in these needs God's will is made clear for those who care for the child. Clearly, some aspects of parenting are much more complicated than this, but even so we should not ignore or forget the obvious.

Likewise with marriage: God's will is that a husband and wife love and honor each other until one or the other dies. God may not have willed for two people to marry only each other (in any manipulative sense, at least), but once they do marry then God's will for them is built right into the institution of marriage itself: making a home, supporting each other in many ways, probably having children and caring for them responsibly, caring for each other in sickness and in health, in good times and bad, cherishing each other—to name only a few things. Of course, in any society, a lot of other (non-divine) demands get built into marriage also, so that many people marry with hopelessly unreal expectations regarding happiness, sexual satisfaction, self-fulfillment, etc. This means that honoring God's will in marriage will involve faithfully sorting out rightful demands from impossible and unwise demands. And if we think of marriage as a calling by God this will help us in our honoring it and sorting out what we are called to do. Even if the marriage suffers an irreparable breakdown, so that divorce finally is judged to be the only possibility, for those who understand marriage to be a calling this action will be taken only after doing everything possible to improve and save the marriage; in that case, even the process of divorce will honor the calling of marriage by being done faithfully.

The point is that we will find God's will in and through the demands and contexts in which we find ourselves. Not that the will of God can be equated with all demands upon us (or opportunities in front of us); many will be anything but divine. Rather, the demands will confront us in our various places and roles in such a way that we will have to ask what is loving and just for the particular neighbors that God has given us in this time and place. And in responding in terms of our being called by God, we will first of all do what our roles and duties suggest or require. We do not have to do some other thing to be doing God's will or working with God.

Questions to think about and discuss:

1. What was your reaction to the various examples that were mentioned of the sorts of things to which God calls people? Were these familiar ideas to you or were they new? Did they make sense to you or not?

2. Sometimes worldly callings seem so ordinary that we wonder why God would even care about them. How do you think about this?

3. While Martin Luther's language about the devil or Satan may seem strange, what do you think about his idea that the devil attacks us precisely in our callings so that we will be tempted to use them only for ourselves and not to serve others?

4. What do you think of the idea that the particular duties, demands, and opportunities right in our roles themselves are things to which God calls us?

5. Do you agree that the belief that God's law is built into what we call "reality" is a helpful way to think about why it is important for us to use all sorts of "secular" wisdom, knowledge, education, and training in order to be faithful and effective in our vocations? If you do not agree, what alternatives might a Christian have?

A classic book on the Christian's calling in the world is *Luther on Vocation*, by Gustaf Wingren; it is challenging but very valuable.

Faith and our Callings

Almost everything we have considered to this point has been about our life in the world, with its needs and activities and with things not normally considered to be religious or specifically Christian. But what about what we often call "the Christian life," the life of worship and prayer, of fellowship and Bible study, of evangelism and acts of justice and mercy? Are we to ignore these things? Sometimes that has been a problem with an over-emphasis on the Christian's worldly vocation—it gets reduced simply to being a good citizen, worker, and family member, while the role of faith in Christ and everything that faith involves gets minimized. Yet without a close and living relationship with the One who calls, how would anyone have a calling? Or, to say it in another way, to live one's life under God's law alone, in the context of our worldly roles and duties, would not sustain anyone's faith, hope, and love.

When we review the origin of the idea of Christians having callings in the world, we realize that it came as a biblically-rooted *corrective* to an emphasis on an overly-religious way of life for Christians, epitomized by certain forms of monasticism. Devoting all of one's life to things religious had led to denigrating God's world and God's ongoing creative involvement in the world. It had "spiritualized" the Christian life in an inappropriate way. ("Spiritual" in this inappropriate view meant primarily *non*-material or *non*-worldly, while "Spirit" in the Bible [i.e., as the breath of God] is related both to the creation of the world, including matter and humans, in Gen. 1-2, and to the incarnation, literally, the "enfleshment" in the world of God's Son, according to the New Testament).

Anytime something begins as a corrective the danger exists that it too will become one-sided if it succeeds and the original problem situation no longer exists. In some instances, that has happened with the idea of worldly callings; people have reduced them merely to occupations or other roles with no sense of God's involvement. Thus many non-believers today will speak of having a vocation. On the other hand, it probably can be argued that Christians and other religious people perpetually are tempted to retreat into the supposedly "spiritual" life (in its non-biblical and anti-material sense). If that is true, it means that resurrecting the idea of worldly callings is important even in an age that is no longer dominated by Christian beliefs and institutions, because it offers Christians an appropriate way of understanding life in light of their faith in Christ.

So, we need to ask what the gospel and Christian faith mean for or contribute to Christian vocation. It has already been stated that God does not intend to govern daily life by the gospel; it also has been said that non-believers actually serve God without knowing it as they carry out their roles and responsibilities. If these things are true, does faith add anything? Does the gospel have anything at all to do with our callings? One way to answer these questions is to look at the experience of Christians in their callings. An immediate answer to these questions for many Christians would be *prayer*. When the going get tough, Christians pray for help. When things are great, Christians thank God. When faced with important choices and decisions, Christians ask God for guidance. When we make wrong choices and act badly and fail, we pray for forgiveness. If we give it some thought, much of our prayer life has to do with our callings —as family members, in relationships, at work, in our communities, at school, in emergencies, illness, and death, for our system of government and public services. (Some people pray every time they hear a fire engine's siren or that of a police car or ambulance; the sound becomes a call to prayer—for the people in the vehicles and for those they are sent to help. And maybe for other things—as long as they are praying anyway!)

Of course, we pray also at other times (for example, at meals, in the morning, before going to sleep, at worship, etc.), but prayer in and for our callings is an important way that our faith in God affects our life in our vocational roles. Prayer reminds us that God cares about who we are and also cares about our neighbors and what we do in our roles. Prayer gives us a true perspective on what otherwise often might seem to be just a bunch of trivial matters. Prayer opens us up to think about God's will for that situation, for those neighbors, and for the larger context. Through prayer God may give us new ideas, may open us up to receive help from others whom we had ignored, or may help us to realize when there is nothing more we can do. Prayer should help us to say "Not my will but thine be done, O Lord." It may lead us to acknowledge our sin and repent. In all of these ways, prayer offers ways for God to become part of the situation that had not been available before—at least not available through us and through and for those whom God has given us.

Without elaborating the following points, we could acknowledge from experience or simply from what we have been learning so far that faith in Christ and the hope that comes with it *motivates* Christians to be fervent in love, dedicated to justice, and generous in mercy. Faith in Christ will affect our *values*, *perspectives*, and *goals*, as it draws on biblical pictures of God's steadfast love and righteousness, of God's passion for the oppressed and for those who are suffering, and of God's desire to seek and save all persons. Faith helps give us *understanding* of the world and of God's will that becomes a factor along with other things we know and learn and teach; this in turn will contribute to our ability to figure out what needs to be done and what we can do about it. Faith brings things into *focus*, it helps us see and perceive more truly—no small feat in a world as diverse as we now see ours to be. Faith may give us *courage* and *selflessness* so that when extraordinary things are asked of someone we will be able to respond. Finally, faith should make us *properly critical* in each situation and role in which God calls us. Sin persists, not least in and among persons of faith. Roles become "old" and self-serving even though once they may have been excellent means of service. Situations often are not what they seem to be and must be looked at with appropriate skepticism. In a culture where so much emphasis is put on material success and individual happiness, faith's critical role is very important in all the areas in and to which God calls us.

The last point calls for some additional comments. With the heavy emphasis on serving God in the roles that are provided in the created world and being guided in doing this by God's law as it is built into these roles, there is a constant danger that we will lapse into a sort of "status quo*ism*." We may simply go along to get along; we will take the path of least resistance (and perhaps most pay)—and it will not necessarily seem wrong since it fits with other roles and responsibilities that already exist. Many people in Nazi Germany excused themselves for their involvement in the persecution of Jews by saying that they were simply doing what they were told to do by their superiors—which was what they had been taught about Christian vocation. However, even the presentation of the law and even the stations and offices of a society can become damaged and perverted, so that sometimes the Christian will need to be so critical that he/she will break the law in the name of loving the neighbor, whether that involves hiding Jews or illegal aliens, speeding while taking someone to the hospital, breaking segregation laws, withholding taxes, taking part in protest demonstrations, using one's position to block unjust and immoral activities that it would be easy to overlook, etc. Often this will involve conflicts between our various callings— as citizen and family member, for example, or as whistle blower and employee, as a friend of people and as one who reports those same friends for child abuse. We should not be surprised at this, however, so it is important to lift up this critical aspect of faith's relation to vocation.

Insofar as the church also is an institution of the created world, it too will share in being part of our service according to God's law. We will also have worldly callings that are part of belonging to the church, whether through volunteering our time and talents to the church's programs and institutional concerns or supporting God's work through the church with our money or trying to help in conflict situations within the church or through it in the larger society. As important as these things are, however, there is something more important. Christians also have a *unique* calling with respect to the mission of the church: that of responding to Christ's command to be his witnesses. Clearly, faith will be of great help in this area and it will drive us more deeply into worship, prayer, and study.

In the context of the present study, however, we need to raise the question of whether bearing witness to Christ has any role in our worldly vocations. If we follow the Bible, we cannot say that God only calls us to our roles in daily life, since all Christians are called to be disciples and to make disciples. (See Matt. 28:16-20 and Acts 1:8, for example.) Confessing our faith in Jesus Christ to all people is essential to being a Christian. It is our unique task, since if believers don't bear witness to Jesus, who else will? None of us could even know about our callings in daily life if we hadn't first heard the gospel of salvation through Christ from someone confessing and bearing witness to that good news to us.

The reason for not dealing with Christian witness as a separate topic until now is that we cannot talk about everything at once—and in this study we are dealing with the Christian's calling in the *world*. However, the matter of bearing witness to our faith does come up in our vocations, so it needs to be mentioned, at least.

Witnessing often comes up in relation to roles and situations that are not at all religious and perhaps not even very meaningful in themselves. Consider the following: I used to go to a barber who was a member of our congregation. Each time I had my hair cut he would tell me that he wasn't a very good Christian because he found it so hard to talk to his customers about his Christian faith. I responded that when I went to him for a haircut my interest wasn't in whether or not he talked about Jesus but whether he gave me a good haircut. I said that his giving me a good haircut was a way of loving his neighbor—me and other people who had to look at me! But he could not agree; his view of God did not really include God's intimate care and concern for all aspects of life, even the hairs on my head. I certainly was not against his bearing witness to Christ, but I think that as a barber his first responsibility to the God who called him was to be the best barber he could be. That in itself is valuable. And, I continued, if he was good enough that people would come back again and again then there might be some very appropriate times when people he has gotten to know well over the years would be able to see his true values or hear of his faith or be helped by him in other ways in addition to having their hair cut. But if he was so concerned with witnessing to Christ that he gave poor haircuts, that would neither serve God well nor would his words be a very credible witness. They might even drive some customers away.

While some situations in our occupations and other worldly callings provide easy and natural occasions to speak of faith in Christ, often this is nearly impossible and sometimes even illegal. To be sure, Christians always must be prepared, when someone calls them to account, to make a defense of the hope that is in them (1 Peter 3:15), but to do this when no one is calling us to account often will be counter-productive and we will be written off as some sort of religious fanatics. Understanding our roles as callings, as divine vocations, however, may suggest some opportunities for bearing witness that are both quite natural and highly effective. Many Christians spend long hours in their callings being with other people who are doing much the same thing—whether that is as a parent taking young children to the playground or working together at demanding or boring jobs. The Christian's values, attitude, honesty, work ethic, and respect for and sensitivity toward others precisely in that vocational situation will be noted by others and may lead almost automatically to the question of how we think about what we are doing and why. Then our witness to our faith in Christ will be natural and appropriate.

Questions to think about and discuss:

1. What things in this lesson were most interesting to you? Why?

2. What things do you think were most important for your particular calling(s)?

3. Did you find yourself surprised or puzzled or in disagreement with anything that you read? What?

4. Have there been situations in your own callings that have demanded criticisms of the role or activity itself or that led you to actions or words opposed to what your role seemed to demand? Have you found times when one of your callings put you in great tension with another? Describe.

5. What do you think about the matter of bearing witness in one's worldly calling as that was proposed in this lesson? Think of some of your own experiences in this regard-whether of good or bad or humorous examples.

For an additional resource, the book *Ordinary Saints* by Robert Benne is helpful.

God's Work on Us

There is one last piece to this framework for understanding our lives as Christians by way of our worldly callings. It is a very important piece but it is usually left out in discussions of Christian vocation. Christian vocation is related to God's *creative* work, as we have seen. It also is related to Christ's *saving* work in that the gift of faith in Christ will affect how we carry out our callings. But does Christian vocation have any relationship to *our own* salvation? Is there an intrinsic relationship between the two or is vocation only the next topic after we have been justified by grace through faith on account of Christ?

By now we know that we cannot relate vocation and salvation by claiming that the good works we do in our callings contribute to our own righteousness before God. We know that although we are believers, dedicated to our callings, we are still sinful even though God has pardoned us. Living as a Christian, we realize, involves some strange paradoxes and tensions. In faith we see that our sin is so radical that no part of us escapes its effects and, therefore, we must rely solely on God's mercy in Jesus Christ. Yet because Christ came not to destroy sinners but to save us, to reclaim and restore us to be faithful creatures, and because we have heard the promise that we are counted righteous for Christ's sake, we are in the situation of being both sinful and yet righteous at the same time — from here to eternity!

At the same time, in daily life, in this time between here and eternity, we can improve our character and abilities as these relate to the common good and we can even grow in our prayer life and faithfulness as we are nourished by God through the gospel, the sacraments, Christian fellowship, and our experiences of God's graciousness to us. On the other hand, we also can and do fall back, slipping into old habits or cynicism, forgetting to pray when things are going well, taking our God-given relationships for granted, discovering ways to forget or ignore our needy neighbors without feeling guilty, depending too much and for too long on our own abilities and growing away from God.

This problem of Christian existence always seems to surprise us, just as we are surprised that life becomes more and not less difficult when we believe in Jesus. At first it may feel as if everything is beautiful when faith comes, but the risen Jesus comes with the gospel and abides in us. As his words and deeds begin to reshape our lives we discover the many disjunctions between what we ought to be in Christ and what we and our world are in fact. Luther speaks of this disjunction as that of being both a "new creation" in Christ and yet still being one with the "old Adam."

The problem throughout Christian history has been how to resolve this situation: how to get the "old Adam," our old sinful self, either sanctified (made holy) or killed off. To sanctify the old sinful self would mean changing it into a new righteous self. This project has been full of illuminating, sometimes promising, and always dangerous insights and practices. Consider the word "sanctification:" Literally, it means "to become holy" or "to be made holy"—and "holy" is above all a *religious* category. In popular usage, however, it often has become related also to *moral* improvement, as each day we seek to become better and better people. While moral improvement is a good thing, when that meaning gets transferred into our thinking about our life in relation to God then sanctification may become *our* attempt to make ourselves holy. When it is linked to our callings, we will be tempted to use our success and effectiveness in them as evidence of our righteousness and holiness before God; and then our focus will be on ourselves instead of being on Christ's gift of salvation and on those whom we ought to be serving.

This way of thinking cannot be correct, however, if salvation is entirely God's doing and not our own achievement. Sanctification fully as much as justification is *God's* doing, for it is the Holy Spirit who sanctifies us, who makes us "holy." At this point, quite unexpectedly, the apostle Paul speaks of our "dying with Christ" and our "being crucified with Christ" (see, for example, Rom. 6 and Gal. 2). He writes that in faith Christ comes to us and becomes our new self, so that "it is no longer I who live but Christ who lives in me" (Gal. 2:21). When we have died with Christ, Christ raises us to newness of life and yet the old sinful self still hangs on. The point, according to Paul, is not to try to make the old self holy but for God to put it to death, so that only the self that is new in Christ remains.

How does God put the old sinful self to death? Following Paul, Martin Luther said that this is a function of God's *law*. Not only does the law tell us what we should do and reveal to us what we have failed to do, but it accuses us of sin, condemns us, crushes us, and finally kills our sinful self. Where and how does God's law do this? Where does this "daily dying" (to use Luther's phrase from the Small Catechism) occur? Much of earlier Christian tradition had said that it occurs in penitential exercises, in prayer, in contrition or sorrow for our sin, in doing things to punish our sinful self. Many people continue to think in this way—and in modern times we have tended to understand it primarily in interior and psychological terms, which are easily linked to a similar understanding of things "spiritual." This usually proves to be only another route to allow sanctification to become a human project and achievement. We put our sinful self to death metaphorically by sincere remorse and repentance.

Luther put it quite differently. He said that sanctification as the putting to death of the sinful self occurs right where we live according to the law, that is, *in our callings in daily life.* Here, the new self in faith gladly loves the neighbor even as the old self is compelled to do so by the demands of the calling. The new self goes to work gladly, to serve the common good and to support her family, while the law of survival forces the old self to do so even against its will and thereby it is put to death a bit each day. Each one of us who is married loves our spouse and we do so gladly; but the institution of marriage sometimes has to force our old sinful self to do so when it is tempted to wander off into selfish pursuits—and here again the old self is put to death a bit each day. We ought to pay our taxes and we do so with thanks for living in a democratic society, while at the same time our old self sends in money only out of fear of punishment. Either way, it should be noted, God's work of governing life gets done even when it is through our old self being put to death.

To use more of Luther's language, there will be a "cross" in every person's life: an instrument to put to death the old sinful self. The problem that developed in the church of the late Middle Ages was that people were taught to take up *invented* crosses in the form of religious practices and devotion that caused much pain, suffering, and inconvenience for the person in question. Luther insisted from scripture that one is not to bear some self-selected religious "cross" in imitation of Christ (after all, Jesus told his followers to take up *their* crosses, not his). Rather, a cross will be laid on each believer, as it was laid on Jesus; and for us, as for him, it will be laid on us *in our callings*. There, in the demand to love our neighbor our old unloving self will be crucified in being forced to do it. In the incredible wisdom and economy of God, the same good work which we do in our callings both gets the neighbor loved and is a means for God's Spirit to sanctify us by putting our sinful self to death.

This is radical and counterintuitive. Sanctification in this sense may not look holy at all. It will be hidden in the chores and stresses, and in the successes and accomplishments, of ordinary life. It may well be hidden even from ourselves;

and that is probably a good thing or we would misuse it as an occasion for self-righteousness. Our true righteousness is not our own in any case, so whether it is evident or not is much less important than whether through us God gets some good accomplished. As believers, we should not go looking for crosses and we certainly should not wallow in suffering or deprivation, or by staying in oppressive or abusive situations. Some Christians have thought that way, but that is simply to make one more thing into a means for self-justification. God will take care of our crosses; we don't need to seek them.

This might seem to be a dark and gloomy way to think about the Christian life; it might sound negative and joyless. It is better described as "realistic," however; that is, as being true to our experience of both sin and grace. More than that, having our sinful self put to death daily, being emptied through the work in our callings in ordinary life, opens us up to live by faith. It makes room for Christ in our lives, it literally forces us to pray many times, out of desperation if not out of faith, precisely because we know ourselves to be called by God in a particular role or situation. This way of thinking about the death of the old self, as a consequence of God's raising us to newness of life and calling us to service, gives us courage to endure when things are bad. In the words of the familiar prayer, it helps us to have the courage to change those things that can be changed, the patience to endure those things that cannot be changed, and the wisdom to know the difference.

To look at it another way, it is often surprising to listen to some devout elderly Christian speak of her Christian faith. She won't speak of her own growth or improvement as much as of how over the years she has grown in the realization of how totally dependent she is on God's graciousness toward her. It's not the case that with God's help she changed her sinful self into a righteous self. Far from it: she will confess that God gave her a new self through faith in Christ.

We might conclude that God's new creation just as much as the original creation is *ex nihilo* (that is, "from nothing"). The old sinful self lives on, to be sure, even if limping and wounded, until that day when in temporal terms we die. Then our dying with Christ, which began at baptism (Rom. 6:3-6), is completed. The old self, Luther said, is a very strong swimmer and will keep bobbing up long after we would have thought it had drowned. And we will be tempted, often, to identify with that self, to try to rescue it and preserve it, instead of acknowledging God's judgment on our sin and clinging instead to God's promise of the resurrection that follows death. Our true identity is in that new life which we know in part even now through faith in Christ and our hope for eternal life. It is this confidence that sets us free to embrace our earthly callings.

Some questions to think about and discuss:

1. Sin is a difficult thing to understand. In the Bible, sin is more than only doing something bad. At a deeper level a bad act is seen to be rooted in a wrong or broken relationship with God; it is something so profoundly wrong that only the crucifixion of God's Son could make things right again. That is why Christian theology must take sin so seriously. In light of that, what were your reactions to the way this lesson speaks about sin and sanctification?

2. What questions do you need to discuss further?

3. Did you think of times in your own life as a Christian when things said in this lesson connected to your experience?

 **Afterword**

There are many more things to think about that are related to the Christian's calling in the world. For example, how might the concept of vocation help Christians to select a way to proceed in further education beyond high school or to choose an occupation? Also, how might God's calling enter into our thinking about remaining single or marrying and, if the latter, about whom we will marry? Another important case, because of the rapid growth of the number of older persons in our society, has to do with discovering ways to understand one's vocation in retirement.

An area that is closely related is ethics: that is, in light of God's calling us in our roles and places of responsibilities, how do we understand what is right or wrong, good or bad, responsible or irresponsible, fitting or inappropriate? The ethics of vocation, as it has been understood by Lutherans, often has been criticized by persons from the Catholic, Reformed, and Evangelical traditions for being unthinkingly conservative or passive or merely secular in its locating faithful actions within the context of our worldly roles and responsibilities. What might we learn from this debate and what might those from other traditions learn from a Lutheran stance? In particular, Christians from the Reformed tradition (for example, Presbyterians) also have devoted much attention to the Christian's calling in the world and Lutheran-Reformed conversations can be very helpful because each group's strengths can rectify some shortcomings in the other group's understanding of vocation.

Feminist and liberation theologians made far-reaching criticisms of most modern Western Christian traditions during the last thirty-five years of the twentieth century. In particular, their criticisms hit hard certain aspects of a vocational approach, especially as it often has seemed to support the status quo in terms of class and gender. What effect might these criticisms have on our thinking about and being involved in our callings?

There are many more matters to pursue also in terms of practical implications for living. An especially effective way of going forward is to engage in discussion with people in the same callings. Congregations might do well to provide opportunities for members and others to study and discuss their callings together. In addition, the resources mentioned at the end of several chapters (above) may be helpful in following up on insights and questions that have been raised. A few additional resources are listed below.

Lee Hardy, *The Fabric of this World: Inquiries into Calling, Career Choice, and the Design of Human Work.* (Grand Rapids, MI: Eerdmans, 1990). Valuable, even though Hardy is better on Calvin than on Luther; a helpful book on the topics in the sub-title.

Paul Ramsey, *Basic Christian Ethics* (Louisville: Westminster/ Knox, 1993 [orig. 1950]). See pp. 153-190 on vocational ethics.

Connections: Faith and Life. An excellent adult study program published by the Lutheran Church in America in 1986 and now available from Center for Lifelong Learning, Luther Seminary.

Marc Kolden, "Christian Vocation in Light of Feminist Critiques," *Lutheran Quarterly* 10 (1996) 71-85.

Marc Kolden, *Living the Faith*, in the "Rejoice" adult education series from Augsburg Fortress Press, 1992.

Marc Kolden, "Work and Meaning: Some Theological Reflections," *Interpretation* 48 (July 1994) 262-271.

See also writings by Marc Kolden on his Web page at www.luthersem.edu/mkolden

About the Author

Author Marc Kolden is professor of systematic theology at Luther Seminary. His research on the doctrine of Christian vocation focuses on some of the core concerns of today's congregations, including lay ministry, Christian ethics, and sanctification.

For additional material on vocation, see his Web page at www.luthersem.edu/mkolden.